INCREDIBLE
CAPTURES

INCREDIBLE CAPTURES

Bill Morgan

SCHOLASTIC INC.
New York Toronto London Auckland Sydney

No part of this publication may be reproduced in whole or in part, or stored in a retrieval system, or transmitted in any form or by any means, electronic, mechanical, photocopying, recording, or otherwise, without written permission of the publisher. For information regarding permission, write to Scholastic Inc., 730 Broadway, New York, NY 10003.

ISBN 0-590-47142-2

12 11 10   4 5 6 7 8/0

Printed in the U.S.A.   01

First Scholastic printing, November 1993

Contents

Contents

Introduction

The men and women who make it their life's work to track down and catch criminals often say their job is very dull. Much of their time is spent going through files. For hours police often go through phone records, applications for driver's licenses, and bank statements. Or they sit hour after hour on a stakeout, waiting for a suspected criminal to appear. Rarely, they claim, is police work as exciting as it is portrayed on television.

But sometimes it is.

Incredible Captures explores five such cases. In these five stories, police and federal law enforcement agents were involved in some of the most exciting captures of our nation's lawbreakers.

And there are incredible captures of all kinds of criminals in this volume: from a gang of hotel robbers, to a murderer, to a drug smuggler.

Bobby Comfort was a master of armed robbery. But banks weren't his targets — safe-deposit boxes in luxury hotels were. Comfort and his gang pulled off the largest hotel robbery in the U.S. at the favorite hotel of then president, Richard Nixon.

John List was a mild-mannered Sunday school teacher until he brutally murdered five members of his family one day in November 1971, at the List home in New Jersey. He escaped authorities for more than seventeen years before being captured.

There were ten men involved with robbing Brinks Incorporated in Boston back in 1950. For almost six years, the "Brinks Gang" got away with the multi-million-dollar robbery. Then just days before the six-year limit on prosecuting robbery cases passed, the cops broke the case when one member of the gang decided it was time to "squeal" on his partners.

Lauren Mahone was just seven years old when her father, who was divorced from her mother, picked her up for a weekend trip. Instead of going to the State Fair in Houston, her father took Lauren halfway around the world to Jordan. Lauren's mother, Cathy, tried every way she could to get her daughter back. Finally, she called an anti-terrorist unit of the United States Army to help her recapture her daughter and return her to Texas.

Johnny Kon was listed in the Hong Kong phone book as a furrier. In truth, he was the head of one of the largest heroin-smuggling rings out of Asia. When detectives began to arrest his drug smugglers in Seattle and New York, the chase was on to capture one of the world's most dangerous drug smugglers.

While police and other law enforcement agencies may, at times, find their work dull, these five cases prove one thing — capturing criminals can be interesting, exciting, and dangerous!

INCREDIBLE CAPTURES

The Capture
of Bobby Comfort

A Thief Is Made

Bobby Comfort began stealing in 1939 when he was seven years old. He didn't stop until 1972, after he and four other men committed the largest hotel robbery in American history.

Bobby's life as a thief began one morning as he was getting ready to go to school. Before he left that morning, his mother called to him. She asked him to go upstairs and steal twenty dollars from her husband.

Bobby's father, Joe Comfort, ran a candy store in Rochester, New York. In the back of the candy store, Joe held illegal card games and made a lot of money on the gambling that went on during the games. Every night Joe Comfort came home with the cash, put it under his pillow, and went to sleep.

Bobby did what his mother asked him to do. He tiptoed into his parents' bedroom and carefully grabbed a twenty from the large roll of bills. Joe Comfort didn't wake up, and Bobby had begun his life of crime. His mother asked him to steal money from under the pillow every week.

It wasn't long before Bobby figured out that he could take an extra twenty dollars for himself without his mother or father knowing about it.

With the money he stole from his father, Bobby took his friends to the local amusement park and would buy them candy and other treats. He soon became the most popular kid in his neighborhood.

By the time Bobby was ten years old, he had decided to rob other people besides his father. With his friend Davey Nelson, Bobby began to rob local supermarkets. The two young thieves would hide behind large empty boxes in the back of the store until closing time. Then, after everyone had left, the two boys would steal food and candy. Since this was before electronic security systems, all the boys had to do was open a back window and climb out of the store.

As Bobby became a teenager, his crimes became more serious. He began breaking into homes and local businesses. When he was thirteen, he was arrested for stealing from a cash register at a gas station and sent to reform school. It was there he learned about carrying a gun and walking into a store and holding it up in broad daylight.

After he served a ten-month sentence in reform school and returned home, Bobby resumed his life of crime. He began breaking into people's homes. In one, he found a .38 revolver. Soon, Bobby and two friends were holding up stores. But their reign of crime did not last long.

One day Peggy Comfort answered a knock at the door to find two policemen and the local grocer asking for Bobby. When Bobby came to the door, the grocer told the police that Bobby had robbed him.

The judge sentenced Bobby to thirty years in prison after Bobby refused to admit to committing the crime. It was a very harsh sentence for a sixteen-year-old.

Surprisingly, Bobby was released on parole after two and a half years. It was 1951, and Bobby had no intention of ever going back to prison.

Bobby had a job waiting for him in an automobile plant upon his release from prison. But working on an assembly line wasn't very exciting, and he soon quit. It wasn't long before he returned to his criminal ways.

For the next several years, Bobby was in and out of prisons. He would win parole and then commit another crime and get caught. In 1959, Bobby hooked up with his boyhood friend Davey Nelson. The two began to break into safes of local businesses after they had closed for the night. Once again, Bobby was destined to get caught.

The two safecrackers decided to break into the safe of one of the largest auto dealers in Rochester. The day of silent burglar alarms had arrived, so when Bobby and Davey broke the windows of the auto dealer's office, they hid nearby waiting to see if the police would come. After fifteen minutes were up, Bobby decided it was safe and the two entered the office through the broken window. A few minutes later, Bobby and Davey were surprised to hear sirens and see a squad of police cars encircle the office. There was no escape.

Bobby was sent to the Monroe County Jail in Rochester. It was not a place where Bobby wanted to stay. As it turned out, he didn't. Before his case came to trial, Bobby plotted an escape from the Rochester jail. With five other convicts, Bobby broke out of prison.

Bobby headed immediately for New York City, but he didn't stay there for long.

Pretty soon he ended up in Jacksonville, Florida, living with his sister, Rosie, and her husband, Joe. It was while Bobby was in Florida that he began to think about robbing hotels. Millie, a girlfriend Bobby had met in Rochester, New York, flew down for a visit and Bobby took her to Miami. They went out to dinner and to see stage shows at some of the nicer hotels in Miami Beach.

Bobby couldn't help but notice that many of the women staying in the hotel wore expensive jewels. Bobby also noticed that the hotels offered to store those jewels in safe-deposit boxes.

To Bobby it seemed like robbing a bank — only easier. He noticed that the safe-deposit boxes were placed right behind the registration desk and that the vault door was often left open. Also, there were no cameras or armed security guards near the safe-deposit boxes. The more Bobby thought about it, the more he liked the idea of robbing hotels.

But he didn't get a chance to carry out any of his plans. Back in Jacksonville, Bobby was caught by police one night when he returned to Rosie and Joe's house. In March of 1960, Bobby was back in Rochester and on his way to jail.

The Hotel Robberies Begin

Once Bobby was back in jail he began to read law books. He found out that the judge in his first trial, the one for robbing a grocery store when Bobby was sixteen, had made a legal error.

Bobby pleaded his case and the court ruled in his favor. It took several years for the legal process to work for Bobby, but by June of 1963, Bobby was once again a free man.

His girlfriend, Millie, had waited for him and the two were married shortly after Bobby's release. Once he was free, Bobby went back to committing crimes. Soon there was another trip to prison for Bobby.

Millie came to visit her husband, but she was beginning to see that his life of crime did not make for an ideal marriage. When Bobby was released from Attica in April of 1969, Millie begged Bobby to get a real job. He agreed.

His sister, Rosie, and her husband, Joe, had moved from Florida to Yonkers, New York. Joe got Bobby a job working on a cement truck for a construction company. Bobby didn't even stay on the job until lunch hour.

A few weeks later, an old friend of Bobby's from Attica called to say that he wanted Bobby to meet someone named Sammy Nalo. Sammy had heard about Bobby, and the two men met to see if they could do some work together. Of course, the work they were talking about was committing robberies.

The two men met in a New York City restaurant, and soon Bobby was telling Sammy about his plans to rob hotels. At first Sammy didn't think too much of the idea. But as Bobby talked more and more about his plans, Sammy began to see where robbing hotels might make more sense than robbing banks.

Soon, the two men began to visit some of New York City's nicest hotels. They would sit in the lobby and check for security guards, see how many people worked the desk, and how easy or difficult it was to get to the hotel's safe-deposit boxes.

Bobby and Sammy began robbing some of the smaller, less fancy hotels in Manhattan. They were always successful and stole enough jewels and money to make a comfortable living. Then they decided to start robbing some of the finer hotels in the city.

The first luxury hotel the pair decided to rob was the Navarro Hotel on Central Park South. Bobby and Sammy got a third person to help them and the three robbers entered the luxury hotel in the early morning hours of September 14, 1969. They wore tuxedos so that when they first entered the hotel they would look like guests returning from an evening out on the town.

They took over the front desk. Bobby stood guard there while Sammy went in with a crowbar and broke open the safe-deposit boxes. The third man acted as a lookout at the front entrance. Since it was the middle of the night, there were almost no guests coming and going. But then a group of fifteen musicians entered the hotel.

The musicians were returning late after playing at a party. They were still in their colorful costumes and were surprised when Bobby pulled out his gun. He led all fifteen men into the restroom on the ground floor and locked them inside.

As Sammy continued to break open the safe-deposit boxes, the musicians started to sing. Their voices got louder — thanks to the tiled walls and floors of the bathroom. Bobby knew that it would only be a matter of time before the singing would begin to wake up the guests on the floors directly above the hotel's lobby. The three thieves made a hasty exit from the Navarro. But not before they had made off with one hundred thousand dollars in jewels and cash.

The police were beginning to realize that there was a band of hotel robbers loose in New York. A special task force was formed to deal with the hotel burglars.

Bobby, Sammy, and other men they hired for the robberies continued to be successful in breaking into some of New York's better hotels. They always operated the same way. Wearing tuxedos they would enter the hotel in the middle of the night and immediately grab the doorman or security guard. Then Bobby would go to the front desk and, putting a gun to the clerk's head, tie him up and gag him with tape. The third robber would keep watch by the front door as Sammy would begin to break open the safe-deposit boxes.

Bobby always stayed by the front desk. If the phone rang he would answer it. During one robbery, a guest called down to request a wake-up call because he had to catch an airplane early the next morning. Bobby told the guest not to worry. Then he went to the clerk and made him promise to make the wake-up call.

Bobby and Sammy never intended to shoot anyone. They just wanted to steal jewels and money from the rich guests that stayed in New York's fancier hotels. They figured the guns would make people do what they wanted them to do.

The police were becoming increasingly alarmed about the hotel robberies. The robbers were obviously professional, and the police thought they wouldn't stop until they got caught. They just didn't know how to catch them. All the New York City Police Department could do was hope that the robbers would make a mistake. A big one.

But Bobby had no intention of getting caught. And despite the police's theory that the robbers would continue to burglarize New York hotels until they were captured, Bobby knew that it was time to hit one more hotel and then quit.

Millie had given birth to a daughter, Nicole, and she was becoming very unhappy with her husband's life of crime. Every time she read about a hotel robbery she knew Bobby was involved. She also knew that if he ever got caught, their daughter would grow up without her father. She pleaded with Bobby to get a regular job. He would nod his head at his wife but would not promise to do as she wished.

Even though she didn't realize it, Millie's words were having an effect. Bobby wanted to retire from robbing hotels. But he knew that if he could pull off one more robbery, he would never have to work again. All he had to do was find the perfect hotel — a hotel that not only had rich and famous guests, but that had many safe-deposit boxes full of jewels as well. In November of 1971, Bobby found it — the Pierre Hotel on fashionable Fifth Avenue.

One stroll through the lobby of the grand hotel convinced Bobby this was the last place he would ever have to rob. All of the women guests were wearing necklaces, bracelets, and earrings — all made of the most expensive jewels. And Bobby knew that they didn't keep those jewels in their rooms at night. They left them in the safe-deposit boxes — the very boxes that Bobby now knew he was going to rob.

The Biggest Hotel Robbery Ever

For the next several weeks, Bobby and Sammy planned the largest hotel robbery ever committed in America. The first thing they had to do was hire three men to help rob the Pierre. Through friends Bobby and Sammy found three men. Their real names are not known — they went by the nicknames City, Country, and Doc.

Once they had found men to help them rob the hotel, a date for the robbery itself had to be set. Bobby wanted the robbery to occur during the early morning hours of January 2, 1972. That night was New Year's Day night, and Bobby knew most guests would be spending a quiet evening in after celebrating New Year's eve the night before. That meant their expensive jewels would be in the safe-deposit boxes.

In mid-December, Bobby checked into the Pierre under a false name. For more than a week he walked through the hotel, sat in the lobby, and noted how often and how long the door of the vault containing the safe-deposit boxes was open. Bobby knew that when the vault door was open the alarm system was turned off. Several times he saw workers from the hotel punch in a code that deactivated the alarm and opened the heavy steel vault door.

Bobby also sat in the lobby late at night and discovered that at about 3:45 A.M. every morning, someone opened the vault door and sat at a desk going over the hotel's financial records. He decided the robbery would take place at about 4 A.M.

Bobby also saw that the morning crew started to arrive for work at about 6:30 A.M. That meant Bobby, Sammy, and their three helpers would have two hours to open as many of the Pierre's safe-deposit boxes as they could.

As Bobby sat in the lobby of the Pierre, planning

the robbery, he was constantly amazed at the number of jewels being worn by the women guests. There was no doubt in Bobby's mind that the robbery of the Pierre Hotel could make the band of five thieves two million dollars each.

As the scheduled day of the robbery approached there was only one worry. In 1972, Richard Nixon was president of the United States and he stayed at the Pierre whenever he visited New York. It was his favorite hotel. For security reasons, no one knew when the president would be staying at the hotel. Even the employees of the Pierre were only given several hours notice before Nixon would arrive. There was a possibility that Nixon might decide to come to New York for the New Year's holiday and stay a couple of days. If that happened, there would be secret service agents all over the hotel. There would be no way that the Pierre could be robbed with secret service men roaming through the hotel.

A couple of days before the robbery, Bobby read in the newspaper that Nixon was staying in Washington, D.C., for New Year's. Even better, on the night of January 1, 1972, Nixon was being interviewed live on television from the White House. Bobby knew he wouldn't be coming to the Pierre. Everything was set.

In the early morning hours of January 2, 1972, a black limousine pulled up to the 61st Street entrance of the Pierre Hotel. It was the only door that could be used by guests and employees between midnight and 6 A.M. All the other doors were locked.

City walked up to the glass door and gently knocked. He said he had a reservation. The guard got up from his chair and opened the door. Soon there was a gun in the guard's face as Country and Doc walked in behind City, closely followed by Bobby and Sammy.

Bobby went to the front desk and told the clerk that he and his group were taking over the hotel. Quickly the band of robbers began to round up hotel guests and employees that were in the lobby and nearby areas. In less than fifteen minutes, the robbers had tied up nineteen guests and employees of the Pierre Hotel.

Country took over the guard's position at the door so that if anyone entered the hotel, he or she could be tied up and put with the other employees and guests.

Sammy began to open the safe-deposit boxes. One by one he pried them open with his crowbar. At first, not many jewels were found inside the boxes he opened.

But as Sammy continued to break into the boxes, more and more jewels came tumbling out. In one box, piles of money were found. Bobby looked at the stacks and stacks of bills and estimated that there was half a million dollars in cash.

For the next two hours, Sammy broke into box after box. During that time only one person came to the door of the hotel. He was quickly tied up and put with the other guests and employees.

Finally, a little after six, Bobby knew it was time to leave the hotel. Sammy wanted to continue working — more than half of the boxes were still untouched. But Bobby insisted, and the thieves started to make their way out of the hotel. With them they took four suitcases crammed with jewelry and cash.

The robbery went off without a hitch. The five thieves went to an apartment where they changed their clothes and split up the cash. Sammy would be in charge of selling the diamonds from the jewelry and getting the money to Bobby and the others when that was done.

Bobby took a train back to Rochester confident that he and Sammy had pulled off the largest hotel robbery ever. There was no way the police would ever catch them.

Capture

The plan was for the five thieves to lay low for about a month. There would be no communication between the five men, and the jewels would stay hidden in Sammy's apartment. No attempt would be made to sell the stolen diamonds for at least a month — or until the heat died down from the largest hotel robbery in history.

The robbery was front-page news across the country. The police were baffled by the crime, but they were determined to catch the thieves.

When Bobby picked up his phone in Rochester a few days after the robbery, he was alarmed to hear Sammy on the other end.

Sammy told Bobby he needed to sell a few of the diamonds immediately. He owed money on some gambling debts and the men he owed that money to wanted it immediately. He asked Bobby to come to New York to help him sell some of the jewels.

The last place Bobby wanted to go was New York. And his instincts told him that selling any of the stolen jewelry so soon after the robbery was just asking for trouble. But he knew he had to help his friend.

Before leaving for New York, Bobby called his friend Dom Paulino and asked him to come along to New York. It would be too risky for Bobby to be there when the jewels were sold so he brought his friend Dom to take his place.

Meanwhile in New York, the police were determined to find the men responsible for robbing the Pierre Hotel. It was hard to determine how much in cash and jewels had been stolen but estimates ran between four and ten million dollars. The police were not going to rest until they found the thieves. Since the police figured the thieves had probably taken the jewels and cash across state lines, making the hotel robbery a federal crime, the FBI joined in the hunt.

When Bobby and Dom got to New York they checked into a mid-Manhattan hotel. Bobby met with Sammy, who told Bobby that he had found a buyer for the jewels. But there was something else to take care of first.

Sammy didn't want to keep any of the stolen

jewelry in his apartment anymore. The extensive coverage of the robbery in the newspapers and on television made Sammy nervous.

Bobby and Sammy decided it would be better for City to hold on to the diamonds. He was still in the New York area. They called City to ask him to hold the gems until the heat died down and they could sell the jewels. City met with Bobby and Sammy. He agreed to hold on to the jewels. City put them in the trunk of his car and drove away.

Then Sammy told Bobby that finding someone to buy the jewels hadn't been easy. The Pierre robbery was big news in New York, and since there was a lot of pressure on the police to find the stolen gems, no jeweler wanted to take a risk handling any jewels thought to be from the Pierre's safe-deposit boxes.

Sammy told Bobby that a friend of his named Bert Stern knew a man named Mr. Towson. Mr. Towson had let Stern know that a certain Mr. Jones would be willing to buy the jewels. Sammy told Bobby he trusted Stern. Bobby met with Stern and Towson. The whole thing didn't feel right to him. But he knew Sammy had to sell some of the jewels to pay his gambling debts. Bobby and Sammy began to plan how the jewels would be exchanged.

Bobby's friend Dom would go to a hotel with Stern, Towson, and a jewelry expert who would determine the worth of the jewels. There they would meet Mr. Jones. Once the expert declared the worth of the gems, Mr. Jones would hand over the cash and then take the jewels. The exchange would be done in room 1554 of the Summit Hotel on New York's east side.

What Stern and the appraiser didn't know was that Mr. Towson was an FBI informant and Mr. Jones was an FBI agent. When Stern had approached Towson about finding a buyer for some jewels, Towson had a feeling that the jewels came from the Pierre robbery. He called the FBI.

On Friday, January 7, 1972, Stern, Towson, Mr. Jones, Dom, and the jewelry expert met in the lobby of the Summit Hotel. Towson and Stern introduced Dom to Mr. Jones. Their job was done. They left the hotel. As soon as Stern walked out onto the sidewalk, two policemen grabbed him and put him in a patrol car. From the backseat, Stern could see Towson walking down the street. The police had not grabbed him.

Dom did not know that Stern had been arrested when he and the jewelry expert went up to room 1554 of the hotel to wait for Mr. Jones. Jones had gone to call "his people" and let them know the jewels were in the Summit Hotel.

"His people" was the FBI. They had been in the room next to 1554 waiting for the call from Mr. Jones. Now they were ready to move.

Dom and the jewelry experts were in room 1554 for just a few minutes when the door was broken down by several FBI agents. They handcuffed Dom and the jewelry expert. They also grabbed fifty-two shiny stones that lay in a white handkerchief.

Bobby was in another hotel waiting for Dom to return with the money. He didn't know that Dom had been arrested, or that Dom had a receipt in his pocket for his and Bobby's hotel room with the room number on it. The FBI found the receipt and decided to check out the room Bobby was waiting in.

When there was a knock on his hotel room door, Bobby tensed. When he asked who was at the door, the reply was the door being broken down. Soon there were four FBI agents, guns drawn, surrounding Bobby.

Bobby was taken to a jail in lower Manhattan. He denied having anything to do with the robbery at the Pierre. But the police and FBI were sure he did.

Sammy was not caught until later that night outside his apartment in the Bronx. Like Bobby, he denied being involved in the Pierre Hotel robbery.

Bobby and Sammy were brought to trial several months later. The only jewels that the police or the FBI had were the ones they got in room 1554 of the Summit Hotel. Many of the diamonds worth millions of dollars were still not accounted for. Bobby and Sammy couldn't tell the authorities where the diamonds were because they themselves didn't know where City had taken them.

At their trial, only one of the hotel employees who had been tied up by the robbers the night of the robbery could identify Bobby and Sammy as the thieves. That witness also identified Dom as having been one of the robbers when he wasn't.

The other problem for the authorities was the

fact the diamonds they got at the Summit Hotel could not be proved one hundred percent to have come from the robbery at the Pierre.

The authorities cut a deal with Bobby and Sammy. If they pleaded guilty, they would get a sentence of only four years in prison for robbing the Pierre Hotel. With good behavior, they would serve two and a half. Bobby and Sammy agreed.

Before Bobby began his sentence he got a phone call from City. City assured him that the jewels were safe and that he would hold Bobby's share until he was out of prison.

Bobby began to serve his sentence on January 3, 1973. It was one year and one day after the robbery at the Pierre Hotel.

Two and a half years later, Bobby was released from prison. Outside the prison gates, Millie was waiting in the car. They went home to Rochester.

Sammy and Bobby did not remain friends. After Sammy was released from prison he was soon caught during a robbery in a Manhattan jewelry store. He was sentenced to almost twenty years in prison.

Bobby retired from his life of crime. He and Millie lived a quiet life in Rochester.

But what happened to Bobby's share of the stolen jewelry? He claims he never heard from City again — and never got his share. Whether that is true or not will never be known. He died of lung cancer at the age of fifty-two on June 6, 1986.

Most of the jewels that were stolen from the Pierre Hotel have never been found.

The Capture
of John List

December 1971: Westfield, New Jersey

Ed Illiano was worried about Patti List. He had
been for a couple of weeks. Patti, a student in
Illiano's drama club, had left with her family almost
a month ago to visit a sick relative in North
Carolina. At first, Illiano wasn't very concerned.
After all, the school had been informed of the trip.
Patti's father, John List, had even told the police
to keep an eye on the List home in Westfield, New
Jersey, while the family was away.

But as the weeks passed, Illiano couldn't shake
the feeling that something was wrong. He began
to drive by the List home on Hillside Avenue
hoping to see that the family had just returned.
The first time he drove by he noticed that every
light in the house was on. Every time he drove by
after that he noticed that the lights were beginning
to go out. It seemed as if, one by one, the lights
in the big house on Hillside Avenue were burning

out. Something about seeing the lights go out upset Illiano.

But even more upsetting was the fact that he hadn't gotten a postcard or letter from Patti while she had been in North Carolina. It just wasn't like her. When the family had taken trips before, Patti had always written her drama teacher a postcard. One time the family just went away for the weekend when Patti wrote Illiano a postcard. It arrived days after Patti had already returned to his drama class.

And now she had been gone for almost a month and not one word. Illiano made up his mind to do some investigating. In fact, he had grown so fearful that he decided to do something quite drastic. On Sunday night, December 5, 1971, he broke into the List home. Illiano didn't want the neighbors to know what he was doing so he parked his car a few blocks away from the house. As he approached the List home, he noticed that more lights had gone out and the house was now almost completely dark. The sight made him feel uneasy, but he forced himself to walk up the front lawn.

Illiano looked more like a burglar than a drama coach as he neared the house. He kept close to the side of the house and tried to blend in with the shrubs and hedges that lined the side of the List home.

At a basement window near the back of the house, Illiano knelt down. He pulled out a metal nail file and wedged it in the frame of the window. It popped open. But he didn't go in right away. He thought for a moment. Should he go into the house? Or should he go home? Maybe Patti and the rest of her family would be back in a few days. But something inside told him to continue with his plan. Carefully he worked his way through the open window and jumped the few feet to the basement floor.

It was pitch-black. Illiano couldn't see anything in front of him. He pulled a lighter out of his pocket and flicked it on. A small glow allowed him to make his way toward the stairs. After he took a few steps his foot knocked against something on the floor. He lowered his lighter to get a look at what it was. To his horror, he saw that it was the List family dog, Tinkerbelle. The dog was dead. Now, Illiano became very frightened. But he knew he had to go on.

When he opened the basement door and stepped into a room off the kitchen, Illiano stopped dead in his tracks. There was music playing. Could someone be home? Illiano stayed frozen in his position for a couple of minutes listening for voices or footsteps. He heard nothing except the sound of his heart pounding in his chest and the music that reminded him of being in church.

As he stood at the top of the basement stairs, Illiano noticed something else. It was as cold inside the house as the December air outside. There was no heat on. Slowly Illiano began to walk through the first-floor rooms.

The soft music could be heard everywhere he went. Illiano walked through the kitchen, the living room, the dining room, and a front room that

21

John List used as an office. Everything seemed to be normal, except for the music and the coldness of the air inside the house.

Illiano made his way toward the back of the house. There was one more room to check. It was a large room with a high ceiling that was called the ballroom. It had been turned into a playroom for the List children.

There was no door separating the ballroom from the rest of the house — just a big, heavy curtain. Illiano pushed it aside and entered the room. Immediately he could smell a foul odor. The room was dark except for one dim light at the far end.

To his right, Illiano noticed what looked like a pile of clothes in a big heap. He went nearer to get a better look. And suddenly he realized that it wasn't just a pile of empty clothes. There were bodies inside. And the bodies weren't moving.

Illiano first recognized Patti's mother, Helen. Then he was able to see Patti's two brothers: John, Jr., and Frederick. Finally, he was able to make out Patti. Illiano began to cry. His worst fears had come true. Patti, her mother, and two brothers were dead. There was no sign of Patti's father, John List, or of Patti's grandmother, Alma List.

Illiano began to panic. He would have panicked even more if he had gone up to the third-floor bedroom where John List's mother, Alma, lay dead. But he just stood in the ballroom not believing his eyes.

Finally, Illiano began to regain his thoughts.

What if someone came to the house? What if it was the police? What if the police arrived and thought he had committed this terrible crime? Illiano knew he had to get out of the house.

He ran to the front door. Before he put his hand out to turn the knob he stopped. He realized he couldn't just run out the front door. He ran into the dining room and opened a window and let himself out. From there he ran the few blocks to where he had parked his car.

Illiano settled himself in the driver's seat behind the steering wheel. But he didn't put the key in the ignition. All he could do was sit in his car and shake.

December 1971: Golden, Colorado

At about the same time Ed Illiano was roaming around the cold and darkened List home in Westfield, New Jersey, a man by the name of Robert Clark was living far away in Colorado. He had arrived in late November and gone to a motel in Golden, Colorado, looking for a job as a cook.

Golden, Colorado, is a suburb of the state capital of Denver and sits at the foot of the majestic Rocky Mountains. When Robert Clark applied for the job as cook at the Holiday Inn, the man who interviewed him thought something was odd.

He noticed that the man asking for the job was very quiet, and rarely made eye contact. Still, Robert Clark was hired and began his job cooking in the motel's kitchen.

From his first day on the job, the people that worked with Robert Clark noticed that he kept to himself. He didn't joke around with them during work and didn't go out with his co-workers when his shift in the motel kitchen was done. And he never talked about himself — his past, where he came from, or where he had worked. It was as if Robert Clark had no past.

But he did. Robert Clark was really John List of Westfield, New Jersey. On November 9, 1971, he had killed his wife, his mother, and his three children. After John List finished murdering his family, he made himself dinner, destroyed every record of his life as John List, and went to bed. The next morning he got up early and drove the family car to JFK Airport in New York.

He parked the car there and then took a bus to the Port Authority Bus Terminal in Manhattan. From there John List had taken several buses to different cities before ending up in Denver and, finally, Golden, Colorado. John List had always wanted to see the Rocky Mountains. Now, as Robert Clark, he could look out the window of the trailer he was living in and see them.

Robert Clark worked and went home and didn't talk to anyone unless he had to. And every day he checked the paper to see if there was a story about a family being killed in New Jersey.

John List no longer existed. He had become Robert Clark. He rarely thought about his life as John List or the murders he had committed. When he did he tried to tell himself that he had done the right thing.

What drove John List to kill his whole family? Well, for years he had trouble keeping a job and the family had run out of money. The bank was going to take away their house on Hillside Avenue, and they would all be homeless. John List wanted to save his family from a life of poverty . . . so he decided to kill them.

Now, living in Golden, Colorado, as Robert Clark he would sometimes go for a walk through the streets and see some young boys playing baseball. Or a teenage girl talking to a friend. Quickly Robert Clark would turn his eyes and walk back to his trailer. There he would sit inside and try not to think about what he had done.

1977–87: Denver, Colorado

For six years John List lived as Robert Clark in and around the Denver area as a cook. After working in motels and country clubs, he was beginning to feel that it would be safe to make some friends, get a better job, and live a more sociable life. No one had ever connected him with John List from Westfield, New Jersey.

In 1975 he joined St. Paul's Lutheran Church in Denver. At first he just quietly attended the Sunday services. Eventually he helped with the bookkeeping, teaching Sunday school, and going to church social events, just as he had done as John List in Westfield, New Jersey. Only now he was the quiet but friendly Bob Clark to the other members of St. Paul's.

In 1977, Bob got a job as an accountant. That was the work he did when he was John List. During his first six years in Denver he missed being an accountant. So finally, Bob went to an employment agency and got a job keeping the books for a large carpet company.

He also moved to a new apartment complex in Wheat Ridge, Colorado, a suburb of Denver. And then he met a woman named Delores Miller.

Bob decided to go to a church social one night and it was there he was introduced to a quiet woman named Delores who had divorced her husband and moved to Denver. The tall quiet man named Bob told Delores his first wife had died of cancer and he had no living family. The two began to date. Soon, Bob moved to an apartment not far from where Delores lived.

Bob and Delores dated for the next several years. They both liked to spend quiet evenings alone or with friends from church. Finally, in 1985, Bob asked Delores to marry him. She said yes.

The two were married in Baltimore, Maryland, at the home of Delores's mother. The marriage took place almost fourteen years to the day after John List had killed his family in New Jersey.

The couple returned to Denver and lived in Delores's apartment. Next door to Bob and Delores lived a woman named Wanda Flanery. She had been friends with Delores for years. She welcomed Bob when he moved in with his new wife. The three socialized often and became good friends.

And then one day Wanda saw something that shocked her. A newspaper she bought at the supermarket checkout, *The World Weekly*, ran a story in 1987 about a man in New Jersey named John List. He had murdered five members of his family in 1971. Included with the article were two photos. One was a photo of John List as he appeared in 1971 at the time of the murders. The other was an updated computerized photo of what John List would look like in 1987.

Wanda couldn't believe her eyes. It was Bob Clark, her next-door neighbor. The eyes, the face, the hair — everything matched. Wanda put down her paper and looked out her kitchen window toward her next-door neighbor's driveway. There was Bob unloading grocery bags from his car. She looked back at the paper and up again at her neighbor. It *was* him. Or was it? Was she letting her imagination run away with her? After all, it didn't seem possible that a cold-blooded killer could be living next door. Especially when he was such a kind and quiet man.

Wanda decided to show the picture to Delores to see what she thought. That night she saw Bob get into his car and drive off. She went right over to talk to Delores.

At first Delores gasped when she saw the pictures of John List in the paper that Wanda showed her. Quickly she read the story about the quiet, mild-mannered accountant who had murdered his family in New Jersey in 1971.

Finally she told Wanda that the man in the paper and her husband really didn't look all that much alike. They simply couldn't be the same man.

Wanda didn't agree. She told Delores to show the pictures to Bob to see what he would say. Delores said she would and Wanda went home.

A week later, Wanda asked Delores if she had shown the photos to Bob. Delores laughed and told Wanda she had thrown the paper out without bothering to show the pictures to Bob.

Wanda thought that Delores knew her husband better than Wanda did and she tried to forget the whole thing. But she couldn't shake the feeling that Bob Clark was really John List. She bought another copy of the paper but she never talked about John List with Delores again.

A few months after that, Delores told Wanda that she and Bob were moving to Richmond, Virginia. Bob had gotten a job there so that they could live closer to Delores's mother in Baltimore. The job was with an accounting firm and, although she would miss Wanda, Delores was thrilled to be moving closer to her mother.

All Wanda could think about was the fact that John List had been an accountant.

1988–89: Westfield, New Jersey

Since the December night in 1971 when the police were called to the house on Hillside Avenue they had been looking for John List. It seemed to them that he had just vanished. They knew he had killed his family. In his office, John List had left a letter to his minister confessing to the crimes. The police wanted to see John List behind bars.

For sixteen years the police had followed leads all over the world from people calling to say they had seen John List. But not one had gotten them anywhere. The police were very frustrated; yet, they continued in their search.

In February of 1988, a man who was working on the case sat down one night to watch a new program called *America's Most Wanted*. Frank Marranca had heard about the show that recreated crimes and showed pictures of the fugitives at large. Marranca also knew that viewers of the show had helped police capture criminals that had been on the loose for years.

The next day Marranca asked his boss if he could approach the producers of *America's Most Wanted* about doing a piece on John List. His boss told him to go ahead. Marranca wrote to the television show and included a packet of newspaper clippings about the John List case.

In July of 1988, Marranca got his answer, but it wasn't the one he wanted. The producers of *America's Most Wanted* thought that the John List case was just too old. Marranca was disappointed. *America's Most Wanted* had become a very popular program and was seen by millions of viewers every week. Marranca kept the idea in the back of his head to approach *America's Most Wanted* another time.

And he did. In January of 1989, Marranca heard that the executive producer of the show, Michael

Linder, would be speaking at a conference in Wilmington, Delaware. He decided to go hear Linder speak and then talk to him in person about the List case.

Marranca and Jeffrey P. Hummel, who worked with him, went to Wilmington to meet Linder. After the producer spoke, the two men from New Jersey approached Linder about the List case. For an hour they talked about John List, his terrible crimes, and the seventeen years they had been trying to catch him. The producer listened. Then he took them up to his hotel room and the three men discussed John List for the next couple of hours.

When the three men parted company, Marranca and Hummel hoped they had a chance to get John List's story on *America's Most Wanted*.

Two weeks later their hopes became reality. Linder had agreed to do a piece on John List. It would air sometime in May of 1989.

Linder was still doubtful whether the piece would help. After all, it had been more than seventeen years since the murders. And the police only had photos of John List from 1971 and earlier. Surely, his appearance would have changed between then and 1989.

It was decided then to hire a forensic sculptor to make a bust of what John List would look like after he had aged seventeen years since the murders. They hired Frank Bender who had already done three busts for *America's Most Wanted*.

Bender began the long and difficult process of

creating an image of John List as he would look in 1989. He studied photographs, talked to detectives that had worked on the case, and even spoke with John List's neighbors from Hillside Avenue. He wanted to get as much information as he could about the quiet, mild-mannered man who had brutally killed his family.

Meanwhile actors were hired to play the List family and in the spring of 1989, the people of Westfield, New Jersey, saw television crews around town filming scenes about the town's most famous murder case.

When Bender finished his sculpture of John List's 1989 head, he took it to the neighbors on Hillside Avenue. They couldn't believe how much it looked like John List — only seventeen years older.

The police, the producers of *America's Most Wanted*, and the citizens of Westfield, New Jersey, began to think for the first time in a long while that they had a good chance of finally capturing John List.

May 21–June 1, 1989: Richmond, Virginia

America's Most Wanted was one of Bob and Delores's favorite television shows. Every Sunday night at 8 P.M. they would sit in the living room of their new house in Richmond, Virginia, and watch the program. But on Sunday, May 21, 1989, Bob and Delores were in Ohio attending the wedding of Delores's sister. They didn't see the broadcast.

But back in Colorado, Wanda Flanery sat down

to watch *America's Most Wanted* with her daughter, Eva, and her daughter's husband, Randy. It was one of their favorite programs, too.

As the story of John List appeared on television screens across the country, viewers were told of the murders of John List and of his more than seventeen years of escape. Finally a photo of John List from 1971 was on the screen. Then, the bust of what John List probably looked like in 1989 was shown.

Wanda couldn't believe her eyes. "That's Bob," she said to her daughter and son-in-law. Eva agreed but Randy wasn't as sure. It just didn't seem possible that the Bob the three of them had known could possibly have committed such a horrible crime.

But then Wanda remarked that if Bob Clark was really John List, her friend Delores could be in serious trouble. Eva agreed with her and Randy went to the phone.

But after talking with the operators from *America's Most Wanted* for a couple of minutes, he hung up. Wanda asked him why. Randy felt that the television program wasn't really interested in catching John List because there was no reward being offered. Eva told her husband to get back on the phone or she would call *America's Most Wanted* herself.

Randy dialed the number again and gave the operator the address of Robert Clark in Richmond, Virginia.

Wanda felt bad about turning in her friend's

husband, but she was now sure that the man who was married to Delores was really a cold-blooded killer.

In Washington, where *America's Most Wanted* took phone tips from viewers, the producers and several detectives working on the John List case looked through the various leads that had been called in from viewers. The calls kept coming in at a fast and furious pace for an hour after the program had gone off the air. All in all, *America's Most Wanted* received about 300 tips on the where-abouts of John List.

By Thursday, June 1, the FBI had gotten around to checking out a lead on a man named Robert Clark in Richmond, Virginia. At about ten o'clock that morning, Agent Kevin August and three other FBI men knocked on the door of a Mr. and Mrs. Robert Clark.

Delores answered the door and informed the agent that her husband was at work. When August told her why the FBI was there and showed her pictures of a man named John List, Delores remembered the photos Wanda had showed her back in Denver. But she assured the FBI agents that her husband was not the man the FBI was looking for. She even showed them a photo from her wedding to Bob in 1985.

But that photograph convinced the agents even more that they had finally found John List. Once again the agent showed Delores the photo of John List. She began to tremble. The agent could see that she was beginning to accept the possibility that her husband was the same man who had killed his family in New Jersey.

Softly, the agent asked Delores for the address where her husband worked. She looked at him for just an instant without saying a word. Then she told the FBI agents where they could find her husband.

Agent August left one of his men behind with Delores to make sure she didn't call her husband to warn him. After the other agents left, Delores sat down in a chair and began to wonder what was going to happen to the rest of her life.

A little after eleven, three agents walked into an accounting office in Richmond, Virginia, where Sandra Silbermann was working at the front desk. The men told her they were from the FBI and were looking for Robert Clark. Sandra became nervous but told the agents that he was in the back office using the copy machine. The agents asked if there was a back door. Just then she heard Robert Clark's footsteps approaching. As Robert Clark entered the front part of the office, Sandra told the agents that this was the man.

When Robert Clark looked up from the papers he was carrying and saw the three men standing there, he stopped dead in his tracks. The room was very still as the agents asked Robert Clark if he was John List. He said no. For another second the room was still. Then the agents went into action.

August and the other two agents grabbed Robert Clark and placed handcuffs on his wrists. Sandra couldn't believe her eyes. Nor could she believe it when the agents told her that Bob Clark was really John List and that he had killed his mother, his wife, and his three teenaged children in cold blood — especially since Sandra often told her husband what a good, decent, quiet man her co-worker, Bob Clark, was.

The agents led their suspect out of the office and to the local FBI office. There, fingerprints of Robert Clark were taken to see if they matched John List's. There was a record of List's fingerprints from when he was in the military during World War II.

All the time that the FBI waited to see if the fingerprints matched, the quiet man in their custody insisted that he was Robert Clark. He denied that he was John List again and again. But when the fingerprints of Robert Clark matched those of John List's prints from his military days, the FBI knew they had their man. After seventeen and a half years, John List had finally been caught.

John List returned to New Jersey to stand trial for the crimes he had committed in November of 1971. But it wasn't until February of 1990 that Robert Clark finally admitted in court that he was, indeed, John List. That spring, John List stood trial for the murder of his mother, Alma; his wife, Helen; and his three teenaged children, Patti, John, Jr., and Frederick. He told the court how he had killed each member of his family — one by one.

On Thursday, April 12, 1990, a jury found John List guilty of five counts of first-degree murder.

Since New Jersey did not have the death penalty when List killed his family in 1971, he was given five life sentences.

Surely John List was guilty in the murder of his family. But what happened to his second wife, Delores? She went into seclusion shortly after her husband's arrest and eventually went to live with friends.

John List will remain in prison for the rest of his life. Delores, the sixth victim, as one FBI agent called her, lives a life of loneliness and sorrow.

Alma List is buried in Michigan, where she raised her son John. Helen, Patti, John, Jr., and Frederick are buried in a cemetery near Westfield, New Jersey. And finally, after so many years, the five victims of John List can rest in peace.

The Capture
of the Brinks Gang

**The Six-Year Search for
Ten Armed Robbers**

There is a playground on Prince Street in Boston.
There are no swings or slides. It is just a big
concrete playground where the main activity is
neighborhood baseball games.

It is doubtful there were any baseball games
being played on January 17, 1950. The weather
was just too cold and too rainy. Even if there had
been a baseball game that day, it isn't as if the kids
playing would have paid any attention to the low
brick building that bordered one end of the park.
Or that they knew that on the second floor of the
building were the offices of Brinks Incorporated.
And that inside those offices were millions of
dollars.

But on January 17, 1950, there were ten men
in Boston that knew all about Brinks. And it was

the day those men decided to go in and try to take the millions of dollars from Brinks.

An Alarming Lack of Security

Brinks Incorporated did one thing: It delivered money to companies. Usually the money was delivered to companies so that they could pay their employees. The company had become famous for its armored cars and had a history of safely transporting large sums of cash for businesses, such as General Electric, since before 1900.

In Boston, the company had its offices on Prince Street. Every night money would be brought to the second-floor office. Once there, it would be divided up and put into bags. The bags were then placed in a huge vault overnight. The next morning the bags of money were loaded into armored trucks and delivered to companies throughout Boston.

Tony Pino was one of the ten men who planned to rob Brinks. As a local thief, Tony knew the company delivered millions of dollars to local businesses. Tony had become curious one day in 1948 when he saw a Brinks truck go into a garage on Prince Street.

Once he knew where Brinks was, Tony spent the next two years planning out just how he, and nine other men, could rob the company of more than one million dollars.

Before Tony started rounding up a gang to help him rob Brinks, he had to figure out if it was possible to break into the offices where the vault was kept.

Tony went to the roof of a building across the playground from the Brinks offices. With a pair of binoculars, he had a clear view inside Brinks. For months he gazed through the windows and could see that most of the employees left between five and six. Tony also saw the men that stayed every night, bagging money and putting it into the vault, until about seven-thirty or eight o'clock.

After watching this same routine for months, Tony was certain it never changed. The next thing to do was to try and break into the offices and see what kind of security there was to guard all that money once all the employees had left.

The parking garage where Brinks kept all their armored cars was also located on the second floor at 165 Prince Street. In the garage there was a door that led to the offices where the money was kept. Tony snuck into the garage to see if he could break the alarm on the door that led to the Brinks offices — and all that money.

After picking the lock, no alarm sounded. Even so, he ran out of the garage and waited for half an hour to see if a silent alarm brought the police. No one arrived. The door was not wired with an alarm system. Tony couldn't believe it.

But that was just the beginning. When Tony began to pick the locks on doors inside the Brinks offices, he found the same thing. Not one was wired with an alarm system. It was too good to be true. All that money and no alarms to bring the police.

All that remained was the vault. Tony wouldn't have been surprised if it wasn't alarmed, either. But he soon found out that it was, and the alarm could not be disconnected. All of a sudden, his idea of a late-night raid on Brinks had to be changed. The robbery would have to take place while the vault was open. That meant going into Brinks while employees were still there counting and bagging the money.

Now that he knew how the robbery was going to be carried out, Tony began to look for a gang of men to break into 165 Prince Street and rob Brinks.

The first person Tony talked to was his brother-in-law, James Costas. Costas was also a crook. He usually didn't go into the place being robbed. Instead, Costas usually acted as the driver of the getaway car.

Another man Tony asked to join the gang was Joe McGinnis. He was a neighbor of Tony's. He ran a small business but also lived a life of crime — mostly selling illegal liquor.

Tony also got a man named Joseph O'Keefe to join the Brinks Gang. Everybody called him Specs because as a kid he liked to eat old bananas — the kind that had brown speckles all over them. At first everyone called him Speckles, but that was soon shortened to Specs. Even as an adult, everyone still called him Specs.

Six more men were brought into the gang. Now it was time to show each member of the gang how easy it was to get into Brinks. One by one he took them into the Brinks offices. Each of the men was amazed by the lack of security at the company.

Tony gave each man a job to do in the robbery. Seven men would go into the offices while the vault was open and grab the money while it was being counted. One of those men would be Specs.

Tony's brother-in-law, James, would be the lookout. From the rooftop across the playground, he would use a flashlight to signal the seven men to proceed to the vault.

Tony would not go in with the seven men. His job would be to stay in the getaway truck and keep a lookout on Prince Street.

Only Joe McGinnis would not go with the other men to the actual robbery. His job was to help the gang prepare for the robbery and to get the guns the gang would carry with them into Brinks. None of the robbers was a killer. But they each knew guns would help convince the Brinks employees to hand over the money.

For almost two years the gang planned the robbery. They even broke into Brinks late at night when it was empty to rehearse the robbery. As 1949 drew to a close, it was time to do it for real.

Getting the Money

On several nights in December of 1949 and January 1950, Tony and the gang went to Prince Street to do the actual robbery. But each time, something went wrong. One night a fire in the neighborhood brought several fire trucks that blocked the getaway streets.

Another night the robbers got all the way up to the second floor and were ready to go into the offices. But Costas did not give the go-ahead signal from his post on the rooftop across the playground. It seems just as the gang made it to the second floor of 165 Prince Street, the Brinks employees shut the vault and set the alarm. Once the vault was closed it was alarmed. Having the employees open it again was too risky.

When Tony saw that the weather report called for light rain during the day and night of January 17, 1950, he decided to try again. All ten men were called and told to be ready to go.

At 5:45 P.M. James Costas left to go to his post on the roof of the building across the playground from Brinks. At about 6:15 P.M. the rest of the gang left their hideout and made their way toward 165 Prince Street in a truck. Someone commented that rain made good robbery weather. People who walked in the streets usually kept their heads down to avoid getting their faces wet or were hidden under umbrellas.

It was a cold night as the gang drove to Brinks. But the long overcoats and hats that each of the seven men wore helped keep them warm. Inside their hats, they also had rubber masks they could pull down once they got inside Brinks. The truck made its way toward Prince Street.

At about 7 P.M. a local nineteen-year-old, Edwin Coffin, went into a candy store across from 165 Prince Street. As he bought a pack of cigarettes his seventeen-year-old girlfriend came into the store. Since the rain had stopped, Edwin suggested to her that they go sit in the playground and talk.

As the teenage couple crossed Prince Street, a truck came racing toward them. Edwin had to grab his girlfriend and push her quickly out of the truck's way. The truck came to a stop. Edwin considered going over and saying something to the driver. He was really angry.

As Edwin approached the truck, it began to back up, Edwin changed his mind and decided to walk away. He turned from the truck, kept his arm around his girlfriend's shoulders, and led her into the darkened playground.

Inside the truck, Tony was furious with the driver for speeding when there was no reason for it. But he soon forgot his anger and ordered the robbery to start.

The men jumped out of the back of the truck and began entering 165 Prince Street. From where he was sitting in the playground, Edwin Coffin saw some of the men jump from the truck. He didn't give it much thought. As they were ordered, the robbers hadn't pulled down their masks yet, so they didn't look odd going into the building. After watching the men go into 165 Prince Street, Edwin resumed talking to his girlfriend.

Once inside the building, the men quietly made their way to the office door. Outside the door, they looked out to the roof of the building across the playground. A light flashed back telling the robbers to proceed toward the vault.

Silently the men entered the offices. Each pulled

down his Halloween-type rubber mask. Each man also carried a plain white laundry bag and a gun.

In the vault room, the men counting and bagging the money had no idea seven men were on their way to the vault. Quietly they counted money, put it into bags, and placed it in the vault. It was just like any other night.

The seven armed robbers arrived where the men were counting the money. They stood there for a moment in complete silence, their guns aimed at the Brinks employees. No one from Brinks looked up.

Finally one of the robbers spoke up. "Okay, boys, put them in the air."

The men counting the money froze. Slowly they lifted their eyes in disbelief at the seven masked men with guns. Then one by one they raised their arms.

The robbers finally moved. They rounded up the employees and made them lie facedown on the floor. Rope was produced from coat pockets and the employees' wrists were soon tied behind their backs. Tape was placed over their mouths. Once the employees were bound and gagged, the robbers walked into the vault and began to put money into their white laundry bags.

For several minutes the masked men grabbed money out of the vault and stuffed it into their bags. They went to the tables where money was still being counted and swept that into their bags. Two of the robbers kept watch over the employees to make sure they remained facedown on the floor.

As the men continued to work, a door buzzer shattered the silence.

None of the gang was prepared for someone to be using a buzzer. One of the robbers took the tape off one of the men on the floor and asked who was buzzing. The employee said it was a guard.

Two of the robbers walked toward the front door. Again the buzzer went off. One robber suggested buzzing him in. The other suggested they wait and see what the guard would do. In a few more seconds, they could hear the guard walking away.

The seven robbers knew it was time to leave.

Carrying their bags, heavy with all the money, the men left the vault room, went through the rest of the offices, and out the front door. Quickly they made their way back to the truck. The robbers threw their laundry bags into the back and began to pile in. The seven men had been inside Brinks less than twenty minutes.

Edwin Coffin looked up as he was talking to his girlfriend. He thought it was strange when he saw seven men come out of the front door of 165 Prince Street carrying full laundry bags. He watched as they all jumped into the back of the truck and the truck roared off. A few hours later when he heard that Brinks had been robbed, he knew he had actually seen the men who had committed the crime. Edwin Coffin called the FBI.

Meanwhile, as the truck rolled through the streets of Boston, the men took off their masks, hats, and overcoats. They were put into an empty bag that would be burned later.

The plan was to get each of the men home as soon as possible to be around family or friends. They wanted to have alibis in case the police questioned them about the robbery. The money would be taken to a safe place. The next day, all ten men would gather to count the money and split it up evenly.

One by one the men were dropped off by their homes. When Tony left the truck he went to his aunt's house. Then, walking home, he ran into a policeman he knew. For Tony, it was a stroke of luck. It had just been minutes since the robbery at Brinks and now he was talking to a cop.

After chatting for a few minutes, he nodded at another member of the Boston Police Department that he knew. The officer later remembered the time to be about 7:30 P.M.

Back in the Brinks office, one of the cashiers was able to twist and turn his wrists until the rope became loose enough to free his hands. He jumped up and pulled the alarm. It was 7:27 P.M. One minute later the alarm company called the Boston Police Department to let them know there was trouble at Brinks. In less than fifteen minutes, there were cops all over the Brinks offices at 165 Prince Street.

The Six-Year Search
It took a few hours for the Brinks employees to determine that more than two million dollars in

cash and checks had been taken by the masked robbers. However, neither the FBI nor Brinks ever knew *exactly* how much was stolen.

What was important to the FBI and the Boston Police was finding the thieves. At first, law enforcement authorities thought that it was an inside job because the robbers had gotten into the offices so easily. Officials from Brinks had to admit that the doors were not wired to alarms.

The guard that had buzzed from the garage during the robbery was questioned again and again. The whole time he insisted upon his innocence. Finally the authorities believed him.

But who was responsible? Many of the members of the Brinks Gang were known to the police from previous crimes. Tony Pino was questioned. But he had been seen by two cops at a time so close to the robbery that the police believed him when he said he had nothing to do with the robbery at Brinks.

The police also questioned Tony's brother-in-law James Costas. In fact, all ten men who were part of the Brinks robbery were suspected by the police and questioned. But the police had no proof. None of the men was arrested.

Even though the police had no proof, they kept their eyes on Tony, James, Joe, Specs, and the other men who had robbed Brinks. They were hoping to catch the men spending large sums of cash.

For Tony and the rest of the Brinks Gang, being watched was better than being arrested. But being watched brought about its own set of problems. There was no way they could begin to spend the money they had stolen. They were even afraid to get together to count the money and split it up.

It was agreed that Joe McGinnis would take the money and find a safe hiding place for it. After some time passed, the men would meet and divide the money evenly.

Since the robbers could not enjoy the money they had stolen, it wasn't long before they needed cash. So they did what they did best: committed more crimes. While committing those crimes, some of them got caught.

Specs O'Keefe was arrested and convicted of robbing two stores. Joe McGinnis was found guilty of selling illegal liquor. Other gang members also ended up in jail.

But years passed without any of the gang being arrested for taking part in the Brinks robbery. One of the gang members died in January of 1955. As time passed, it looked as if the men who had robbed Brinks would get away with their crime.

The authorities had until January 17, 1956, to break the case. After that, the statute of limitations would be in effect. In other words, if the police or the FBI had not charged anyone within six years of the crime itself, the robbers could not be arrested for robbing Brinks. As yet, no suspects could be named, and the police were getting desperate.

As that fateful day approached, the police began to get their break. Specs O'Keefe was mad and he was getting ready to talk. He felt he had been betrayed by the other gang members, especially Joe McGinnis.

Joe had never split the money as the gang had agreed. Some of the robbers got some money from him, but Specs felt he had been cheated.

Finally, on January 6, 1956, *just eleven days before the statute of limitations ran out*, Specs O'Keefe called two special agents, John Larkin and Edward J. Powers, to the jail where he was serving time. And on that day, Specs O'Keefe began to talk.

He described the scene to the agents and admitted his guilt in the robbery. Then he named, one by one, every member of the Brinks Gang.

A few days later, the FBI rounded up six of those men. Tony Pino was at home having lunch with James Costas on January 11, 1956. It was about noon. The two men had just sat down to eat when FBI agents entered the house. The two men went quietly.

Joe McGinnis was working in his liquor store when two men in business suits showed up to arrest him for his part in the Brinks robbery. He also went quietly.

In less than ninety minutes, the FBI had captured six of the ten men. Two of the robbers had somehow been tipped off to the arrests and escaped. The FBI knew the other member of the gang had died a year earlier.

Five months later, the two Brinks robbers still at large were caught in an apartment outside of Boston. More than six years after their crime, the Brinks Gang was behind bars.

On June 4, 1956, another member of the gang died of natural causes at the age of thirty-six. There were eight of the ten men left. Those eight men went on trial in August of 1956.

The key witness for the prosecution was Specs O'Keefe. He was delighted to spend days on the witness stand telling a packed courtroom about how the robbery had been planned and carried out.

In detail, Specs told how the robbers broke into Brinks time and time again to look the place over. Everyone in the courtroom seemed amazed that the doors had not been wired to an alarm system. Specs then outlined what each man's role in the robbery had been.

As Specs testified from the stand, the seven other members sat at the defense table in stony silence. They had all entered pleas of "not guilty." And they all refused to take the stand in their defense.

While Specs was the star witness for the prosecution, there was also a surprise witness. Edwin Coffin, the young man who had been in the Prince Street playground the night of the robbery, was called to the stand.

With quiet determination, Edwin told how he and his girlfriend, who had become his wife, were crossing Prince Street the night of January 17, 1950. Edwin told the court how he and his girlfriend were almost run down by a truck. Coffin then said that he watched the men enter 165 Prince

Street as he and his girlfriend were talking in the playground.

Perhaps his most damaging testimony was when he described the gang's getaway. Coffin told the court that as the truck left the scene of the crime, it began to go very fast. And when it turned the corner, the truck looked as if it were going to tip over.

Edwin's testimony backed up what Specs had said earlier in the trial. After the robbery, Specs had jumped into the back of the truck with the other six gang members who had been inside Brinks. As the robbers began to take off their masks and overcoats, he noticed how fast the truck was going. Specs testified that he had felt the truck was going to go over on its side when it turned the corner leaving Prince Street.

Edwin's testimony, along with that of Specs and the Brinks employees, made for a pretty clear-cut case against the Brinks Gang.

On October 6, 1956, the jury got the case. It didn't take them long to come to a verdict. All eight defendants were found guilty.

Three days later, Judge Felix Forte handed down life sentences to every one of the robbers except Specs. For giving state's evidence, Specs was given a lighter sentence that added up to twelve years for armed robbery, breaking and entering, and breaking general laws.

Pino, Costas, McGinnis, and four other members of the gang were sent to Walpole State Prison in Walpole, Massachusetts. Specs was sent to Middlesex County Jail in Cambridge, Massachusetts. The Brinks case was finally closed.

It had taken six years and an estimated $29,000,000 to catch and convict the Brinks Gang. They had stolen an estimated $2,700,000.

Specs was paroled from jail in 1960. He moved to the West Coast where he worked as a seaman, cook, and a chauffeur. He never returned to Boston. On March 4, 1976, Specs O'Keefe died of a heart attack.

James Costas was paroled in 1969 — almost fourteen years after being sent to jail for the Brinks robbery. He returned to his family and became a watchmaker. But soon he returned to a life of crime. In 1975, James Costas was found guilty of counterfeiting more than $1,000,000 in twenty-dollar bills and was sent back to prison.

Joe McGinnis never made it out of jail. He was kneeling in prayer in his cell on October 5, 1966, when he fell over and died.

Tony Pino remained in jail until July of 1971. Upon his release he worked as a janitor in a store. He claimed he only received $89,000 of the Brinks money. Whether he was telling the truth will never be known.

One October night in 1973, Tony Pino walked into his kitchen. His stomach didn't feel right. He sat down in a chair, had a heart attack, and died immediately. When he died, law enforcement officials were not sure what happened to most of the money stolen in 1950. To this day, it has not been found.

The playground still exists next to 165 Prince Street. Today, as kids play baseball or teenagers go to meet and talk, it is doubtful they know they are sitting in the shadow of where the famous Brinks robbery took place on January 17, 1950.

Brinks no longer has its offices on Prince Street in Boston. But before it moved, the company made one improvement. On January 18, 1950, Brinks put alarms on all the doors at 165 Prince Street.

The Capture of Lauren

How a Mother Got Her Daughter Back

Cathy Mahone was desperate. Her seven-year-old daughter, Lauren, had been kidnapped by her ex-husband, Ali Bayan. Her ex-husband hadn't taken Lauren to the next town or the next state. Ali Bayan had taken the child halfway around the world to his homeland of Jordan. Cathy knew he would never bring her back to Dallas, Texas. And the United States government couldn't help her. Cathy Mahone's only chance was to get her daughter back herself.

That is why in December of 1987, Cathy Mahone was sitting in a motel room with Dave Chatellier and Don Feeny. Both men had been a part of the Army's antiterrorist unit, Delta Force. The unit was known for going into foreign countries and rescuing Americans being held against their will. The two men listened to the desperate mother's story.

As Cathy pleaded with the two men to help her, she also said there had to be two rules. The first rule was that no guns could be used. The second rule was that Cathy would be part of the rescue team.

The two men looked at each other. It had not been an ordinary kidnapping. Now, Dave Chatellier and Don Feeny knew it would not be an ordinary rescue.

Dating, Marriage, and a Kidnapping

In the fall of 1975, Cathy Mahone was a nineteen-year-old college student in Dallas, Texas. She had just moved to Texas from her home in northern Florida to attend school. To help pay for her college education, Cathy was working as a waitress at the Country Skillet restaurant.

Ali Bayan was also a college student. He had come to America from his native country of Jordan to get a college education. Ali also worked in the Country Skillet as a waiter and a dishwasher.

Cathy noticed the dark-haired man with the dark eyes looking at her. She said yes when he asked her out. He was kind and thoughtful on their dates and often brought her flowers and other gifts. Cathy started to really like the young man from Jordan. She even took Ali to meet her parents. They liked him, too. He seemed to really care for Cathy.

In June of 1976, eight months after Cathy and Ali started to date, they were married. The couple settled in as newlyweds. Ali turned out to be the same kind of husband he was as a boyfriend — thoughtful and caring.

Ali wanted to take Cathy to meet his family in Jordan. Finally in 1979, the couple was able to afford the trip.

Arriving in Amman, the capital of Jordan, Cathy was immediately impressed. One of Ali's brothers was a doctor for the Jordanian royal family. He was able to get them through customs without delay and on their way to Ali's family in Jarash.

The town of Jarash was filled mostly with homes and local businesses. It was forty-five miles away from Amman, and Ali's family had two houses in the city. Ali's father had been married twice and Ali was one of twenty-four children. There were many relatives to meet.

Cathy found the land of her husband interesting. Just beyond the city were ancient ruins from when the Romans had ruled this part of the world.

Cathy also found it amazing that the streets of Jarash had no names, and the houses had no addresses. The people of Jarash knew where everything was and how to get there. But an outsider could easily get lost.

Soon Cathy began to notice something different about her husband. He was ignoring her. He spent all his time with his brothers. At first it didn't bother her. She knew it had been a long time since they had all seen each other.

When Cathy began to notice that Ali not only ignored her, but all of his sisters, she began to watch more closely. What she saw was that none of the men in Ali's family paid any attention to any of the women, except to tell them what to do. Cathy didn't like it, and she was glad when it was time for her and Ali to go back to Texas.

Once Cathy got back to Dallas, she didn't give the matter too much thought. Ali once again became a kind and attentive husband. Then Cathy found out that she was going to have a baby.

What should have been good news for the young couple turned out to be the beginning of the end of their marriage. Ali went back to Jordan and didn't return to Dallas until just weeks before Cathy gave birth.

Barbara Lauren Bayan was born in 1980. Ali announced that he wanted the little girl he and Cathy called Lauren to be raised in the custom of his Islamic culture. And he wanted her to be raised in Jordan. Cathy couldn't go along with it. They had never planned on moving to Jordan.

The couple argued constantly. It was as if Ali had changed overnight. Six weeks after Lauren was born, Cathy knew her marriage was over. She filed for divorce. On December 30, 1980, Cathy was given a divorce from Ali. The court awarded custody of Lauren to Cathy.

Ali was allowed to visit Lauren. But in the first few months he rarely made the effort to see his daughter. Ali met a woman from Jordan who was living in America and married her.

Cathy had opened her own business and it became more and more successful. She hardly ever saw Ali. Then, all of a sudden, Ali began to visit

Lauren more and more. He would take her to the movies, the circus, or to his new home in Dallas.

Cathy was glad to see Ali and Lauren spending more time together. After all, they were father and daughter. One day Ali asked Cathy if he could take Lauren to meet his family in Jordan. Cathy hesitated at first. Then she admitted to herself that Ali had become a good and loving father. She agreed to let Ali take Lauren to Jordan for a two-week trip.

But when Ali and Lauren didn't return from Jordan after two weeks, Cathy became alarmed. She began to call Ali at the family home in Jarash. Finally, a month after they had left on their trip to Jordan, Ali and Lauren returned to Dallas. After a while, Cathy put the incident out of her mind.

While Ali remained a good father to Lauren, he was having problems in other areas. He had become an owner of the Country Skillet restaurant and business was poor. The restaurant was about to close.

He had also spent thousands and thousands of dollars on his credit cards. And he wasn't planning on ever paying the bills. He had even bought a Honda motorcycle and had it shipped to Jordan on a freighter.

Cathy didn't think anything was unusual when Ali came to pick up Lauren on November 1, 1987, to take her for a day trip to Houston. On that Sunday morning Cathy waved good-bye to her daughter as Lauren and Ali drove off.

Ali was to keep Lauren until after school on Tuesday. At lunchtime on Monday, Cathy began to miss Lauren. She decided to go have lunch with her daughter at Lauren's school.

When Cathy arrived at the school, she was told that Lauren had not shown up for classes that morning. Cathy's stomach sank. She knew something was terribly wrong.

She tried to call Ali at his home. There was no answer. She called his brother. Ali's brother told Cathy that Ali was in New Jersey. When Cathy asked why Ali was in New Jersey, his brother told Cathy that Ali and his second wife had moved there.

Cathy made one more call and her worst fears became real. She called Alia, Jordan's national airline. She found out that Ali and Lauren had been on a Sunday evening flight to Jordan.

Frantic, Cathy called Ali's house in Jordan. No one would talk to her. Lauren was with her father halfway around the world, and Cathy knew he had no intention of bringing her back.

Getting Lauren Back

Cathy was devastated that her ex-husband had taken Lauren to Jordan. She immediately filed a suit with the Texas state courts. A warrant for Ali's arrest was issued by a grand jury. But it meant nothing.

If Ali had taken Lauren to another state, like New Jersey, that state would gladly return Ali to Texas to face criminal charges. But Ali had taken

Lauren to Jordan. It was a whole different story.

There was no agreement between the United States and Jordan to hand over criminals. Besides, Ali had not broken any Jordanian laws. In Jordan, fathers are usually given custody of the children when there is a divorce.

Cathy had pleaded her case to the grand jury, but its hands were tied. A member of the grand jury felt bad for Cathy. He had listened to her story but also knew that there was nothing the court could do to make Ali bring Lauren back to America. He went up to Cathy and handed her his business card. His name was Al Zapanta, and he told Cathy to call him if he could be of help.

First Cathy wanted to try the U.S. Embassy in Jordan. To her amazement she found out that there wasn't much the embassy could do. They could ask the Jordanian government to have Ali Bayan hand Lauren over to American officials. But they knew it wouldn't happen. Already there were more than 500 American children in Jordan who had been kidnapped by their fathers. Cathy also tried the FBI. Sadly, there was nothing they could do, either.

Cathy didn't know where to turn. She even thought of going over to Jordan herself and grabbing Lauren right out of Ali's house. Her friends talked her out of that because of the danger.

Finally she called Al Zapanta. He had an idea.

Al Zapanta had been in the Special Forces during the Vietnam War. He knew some men from Delta Force, an antiterrorist unit, who might be

60

able to carry out a mission to rescue Lauren.

Two weeks after Ali had taken Lauren, Cathy was sitting with Don Feeny and Dave Chatellier in a motel not far from the Dallas/Ft. Worth Airport. Zapanta had gotten in touch with the two men and asked them to meet with Cathy.

They listened to Cathy's heartbreaking story, and to her demands that no guns be used and that she be part of the rescue mission.

Don and Dave had never attempted a rescue like the one Cathy needed to get her child back. It would be risky. This was not a government-approved mission. If anything went wrong they could end up in jail, and the United States government might not be able to help them.

But Cathy impressed them. She had brought pictures of Ali's house and his family, and had given the men detailed accounts of day-to-day life in Jarash.

The men gave the idea a lot of thought. There were problems. Neither man was familiar with Jordan or spoke Arabic. Jarash was not a tourist town — they would stick out as foreigners. And if they got caught, they would be on their own.

But both men had children of their own. They just couldn't turn Cathy down.

The next morning Don and Dave told Cathy they would try to rescue Lauren. They warned her it would be dangerous and there was no guarantee the mission would be successful. Cathy couldn't think about that. All she cared about was that she finally had a chance to get Lauren back.

The first thing Don and Dave did was get a third man to help with the mission to rescue Lauren. He was James Roberts, a man they knew from their days in Delta Force.

The three men began to plot their rescue mission. The first part of the plan didn't involve the three men at all. It involved Cathy.

They told her to call Ali every day. Each time she called she was to sound helpless to her ex-husband. She was to cry and beg for him to bring Lauren back.

Cathy did just that. She would call Ali and beg him to bring Lauren back. When he refused, she would begin to cry and act as if she was so upset at the loss of her daughter she couldn't think straight. If Ali thought Cathy had turned into a total mess, there was no way he would consider she was planning to get her daughter back.

Before the three men left for the Middle East in December, Cathy gave them pictures she had taken when she was in Jordan with Ali soon after their marriage. In one picture, Cathy was sitting on the roof of Ali's house. In the background of the picture were the famous ruins that had been there since the Romans had been in power many centuries before. Since the streets had no names, the photo might help the men find Ali's house and Lauren.

Don, Dave, and James left for Jordan on December 27. Once they arrived they pretended they were from Hollywood and had come to Jordan to look for locations where they could shoot a movie.

Immediately upon arrival in Jarash, the men began to look for Ali's house. They walked the unnamed streets of Jarash trying to find the angle of the photo that had the ruins in the background.

When they thought they had found it, Dave began to sit in a car across the street and watch the house for signs of Ali or Lauren. He also noticed there was a police station behind the house and an army post up the street. Breaking into Ali's house and grabbing Lauren would be too dangerous.

As he watched the house he also noted that no one that came in or out of the house looked like Ali or Lauren. He began to wonder if he had found the right house.

Dave also noticed something else. In the mornings, children did not go out by themselves to wait for the school bus. Seconds before the bus arrived, an adult would bring a child out to the curb just in time for the child to get on the bus. An adult was always waiting at the end of the day to walk them the few yards back into the house when they got off the bus.

Back in Texas, Cathy continued to call Ali and beg for Lauren's return. When Ali refused, she begged him for information. Ali told her that Lauren was going to a special school where she was learning to speak Arabic.

A couple of times, Ali even put Lauren on the phone. Lauren told her mother she rode an orange school bus every day and that she was the tallest one in her class.

In January, Cathy got on a plane for the Middle East. By the time Cathy arrived, Dave had found out exactly where Lauren was going to school. It was a private school right in Jarash. He had parked by the school and seen Lauren on the orange school bus.

The first thing Cathy had noticed when she arrived in Jarash was how much the town had changed. The city was much bigger than it had been nine years before. There were more streets and more people.

When Dave took her to the house that he thought belonged to Ali, Cathy realized she had made a mistake. The house in the photo where she sat on the roof was not Ali's. It was his aunt's house. Dave had been watching the wrong house.

Cathy tried to remember where Ali's house had been in relation to his aunt's. She remembered that there had been a drugstore on the corner of Ali's street. They drove by drugstore after drugstore, until Cathy finally saw one that looked familiar. She knew Ali's house was close by.

As they drove toward where she thought Ali's house was, Cathy got very nervous. Then she saw the motorcycle she knew Ali had bought with his credit card. When she spotted two men standing near the motorcycle, she recognized one of them as her ex-husband. Cathy slid down in her seat so Ali wouldn't see her. But she had recognized his house. The next morning Dave drove over there to watch the house. Sure enough, Lauren was brought out of the house just as the orange school bus pulled up.

As it turned out, Lauren only lived a short distance from her school. Less than the length of a football field. But she took the bus to school every day — as did all the children in Jarash. Jordan, like other Middle Eastern countries, was afraid of terrorist acts, so parents did not allow their children to walk to school no matter how close they lived to it.

Dave watched as a woman brought Lauren out just seconds before the bus stopped in front of the house. Lauren got on and the bus continued on its way to pick up other children. The bus drove to the edge of Jarash, picking up children, and then returned on the same road where it had picked up Lauren to drop the children off at school. The trip took twenty minutes. It would have taken Lauren less than five minutes to walk to school.

Now that the men knew the routine of the school bus, it was decided that they would grab Lauren off the bus on her way to school one morning. At the outskirts of town, the bus had to go up a hill to a farmhouse where two children who took the bus lived. At the top of the hill the bus had to turn around to come back down. It was there the men decided they would block the bus before it turned around on the narrow road.

In addition to taking Lauren off the bus, an escape route out of Jordan had to be planned. Dave, Don, and James figured the best way out of the country for Cathy and Lauren would be through the Israeli-occupied part of the West Bank. From there, they could get to an airport in Israel for a flight to the United States.

Another part of the plan went into action. Dave, Don, and Cathy dressed themselves up as American tourists. For a few days, with cameras around their necks, they would talk to the border guards and tell them all about their vacation in Jordan and their plans to visit Israel soon. They wanted the guards to recognize them as American tourists when they finally had Lauren in hand and were trying to cross the border. After a few days the guards began to smile when they saw Dave, Dan, and Cathy approach. Everyone would chat for a few minutes and then wave good-bye.

Cathy also made fake airline reservations for herself and Lauren from the airport in Amman. She wanted Ali and the police to be searching the Amman airport while she and Lauren were escaping into Israel.

The time had come. On January 28, 1988, Don Feeny sat in a white car outside Ali's house to make sure Lauren got on the bus. Once she boarded, Don sped to the farmhouse where James and Cathy were waiting. They were wearing traditional Arab clothing of long robes. Cathy wore a veil. Under their robes they wore their American tourist clothes.

As Don arrived at the dirt road near the farm, Cathy and James jumped into the car. Dave was nearby in a red car. As the bus arrived near the top of the hill, Don, James, and Cathy drove up the narrow road and came to a halt behind the bus so it couldn't turn around.

The three jumped out of the white car. Don grabbed the driver through the window. He put an envelope in his hand and told the driver to deliver it to Ali. In the envelope was a message from Cathy. It told Ali that she was taking Lauren back to America and for him not to try to get her back.

As Don gave the driver the note, James kicked in the door of the bus and went in. Cathy followed close behind.

Once on the bus, Cathy saw Lauren immediately and ran to her. Lauren's eyes grew huge as she saw her mother come toward her. Cathy picked up her daughter and made her way back to the front of the bus. The other children just looked on in silence.

Don grabbed the keys of the bus and threw them into a field. Cathy ran to the car carrying Lauren and put her in the backseat. An adult supervisor who rode the bus with the children grabbed Cathy as she was putting Lauren in the backseat. Cathy pushed the woman away as Don and James got in the front of the car, started it, and roared down the hill.

Dave was waiting around the corner at the bottom of the hill in the red car. A switch was made. Don, James, Cathy, and Lauren got into the red car as Dave got into the white car. Dave headed back to the center of Jarash in the white car. The red car headed for the Israeli border.

Once inside the car, Don, James, and Cathy took off their Arab clothes. They placed the garments in a bag and tossed it out the car window at some children who were playing by the side of the road. In less than an hour they hoped to be seeing their friendly border guards one more time.

Dave didn't get too far before he was stopped by the police as he drove through Jarash. When several police cars surrounded his car, he was sitting behind the wheel eating a candy bar. He, too, looked like an American tourist.

He told the police he was a tourist on his way to the Dead Sea. They didn't believe him. They searched his car but didn't find anything that connected him to the incident with the school bus.

Finally the bus driver was brought to the car. The driver took one look at Dave and told the police he had not been one of the men who had blocked the bus. While the police were still asking Dave questions, a report came over their radio that Cathy and Lauren were booked on a flight out of the airport in Amman. The police let Dave go and rushed to the Amman airport.

Meanwhile, Don, James, Cathy, and Lauren drove toward the Israeli border. They still weren't sure that they would get past the border guards.

When they finally reached the border they saw their plan had worked. The guards smiled and waved them through the border station. It looked as if they were home free.

Back in Jarash, Dave also headed for the Amman airport. When he arrived, he found that all flights, except one to Paris, had been canceled. There were many police at the airport looking for Cathy and Lauren. Dave walked past them and bought a ticket on the flight to Paris. The next day he took another plane. This one was back to the United States.

Cathy and Lauren also returned to the United States. They returned to Texas. But since they have been back in America, Cathy has taken Lauren and gone into hiding.

Ali was furious that Lauren was recaptured. He asked the United States government to return his daughter to Jordan. The American government has refused. Ali cannot come back to America himself to try and get Lauren. He would be arrested for kidnapping and outstanding bills on his credit cards.

But Ali's brothers can come to America, and that is why Cathy remains in hiding. She lost her daughter once. She doesn't want it to happen again.

The Capture
of Johnny Kon

A Not-So-Routine Drug Bust
The city of Seattle was having a beautiful early
summer day on Sunday, June 23, 1985. And
Special Drug Enforcement Administration (DEA)
Agent Ed Madonna (he knew all the jokes) was
taking advantage of it. Ed was working in his
garden and enjoying turning over the dirt in his
hands as he planted and weeded. He was in such
a good mood that when the beeper of his pager
went off, he got up without complaint and went
into his house to call the office.

Agent Madonna was told that two men had been
arrested for trying to smuggle heroin into Seattle's
airport. The flight had come from Tokyo, and the
two men were being held by customs police. Madonna told his wife he didn't expect to be gone
long. It sounded like a routine bust.

When Madonna arrived at the Seattle–Ta-
coma Airport, he was surprised to see United States

Customs inspectors using drills on 138 metal ice buckets. As the inspectors drilled, heroin began flowing out of the hollow space between the outer metal casing and the insulation wall. By the time they had finished, there were 212 pounds of heroin on the tables around the ice buckets.

Then Madonna learned that one of the two men who had been arrested had already escaped. Claiming he needed to go to the bathroom, one smuggler had been allowed to go into the restroom by himself. When inspectors finally went in to find him, they saw a small window was open. On the floor was a fake mustache. The smuggler had vanished.

Madonna groaned at his bad luck. At least they still had one of the men who had brought in the ice buckets. His name was Tommy Chen. He told Agent Madonna that his instructions had been to take the ice buckets to Chicago, check into the Hilton Hotel, and wait for a phone call. Chen claimed he didn't know the buckets contained heroin.

Madonna was sure that Chen was lying. He offered the smuggler a deal. If Chen would testify to who was running the drug-smuggling operation, the agent would do his best to get the twenty-year jail sentence reduced.

Chen refused to go along. The reason? He knew he would be killed. So would his family. Finally, Chen agreed to go to Chicago with the agents and take the phone call. But he still refused to testify against whomever had hired him to bring the heroin to Seattle.

At the Hilton Hotel at Chicago's O'Hare Airport, Chen was put into a room with an armed guard. Madonna was in the next room. More guards were posted outside the room where Chen waited for the phone call.

At about 11 P.M., the armed guard left Chen for a moment and went to speak with Madonna in his room. As they were talking, they heard a loud crash next door. Running into Chen's room, Madonna saw that he was gone. He had somehow broken the hotel's sealed window and stepped out. It was a long step.

As Madonna looked out the window, he saw that Chen had landed six floors below on a concrete ledge. Madonna couldn't believe his eyes as Chen got up and jumped another two floors to the street. From there, Chen somehow managed to get up and disappear down the street.

Madonna knew then that Chen wasn't kidding. If he was willing to risk his life to jump six stories, Chen feared he would never live to testify. Madonna notified the local police that Chen was on the loose.

About 11:30 P.M. a police officer saw a man bleeding and having a hard time walking trying to get on a bus to New York City. Chen was taken back to Madonna.

Chen had fractured his ankle and suffered internal injuries. But still, he would not tell Madonna who had hired him to smuggle the drugs.

Who's the Boss?

Back in Seattle, Madonna had a feeling that the bust of 212 pounds of heroin was just the tip of the iceberg in terms of drugs coming into America. He went through all of Chen's travel documents and discovered that the smuggler who had gotten away was Fang Han-Sheng.

Madonna ran the names of Chen and Fang Han-Sheng through a computer that kept customs forms everyone must fill out each time they visit the United States. The computer showed that Chen and Han-Sheng had come to the States many times in the past two years. Sometimes they came together and sometimes they came with other smugglers. And they were coming from many different cities in the Far East.

Madonna now knew this was a huge smuggling operation. But who was the boss? He was determined to find out.

Agent Madonna contacted DEA offices around the world. They could offer little help because they were swamped with cases of their own. Then something happened.

Han-Sheng, the drug smuggler who had gotten away from customs officials in Seattle, was found shot to death in Bangkok, Thailand. The murder was in the style of professional drug dealers killing one of their own.

Madonna went to talk with DEA agents in Thailand. There he met John Pritchard, an agent from Hong Kong, and the two men began to work together. They looked over passports and other documents Thai authorities had found when Han-Sheng was killed.

Pritchard immediately recognized names and faces of smugglers from a drug bust in Hong Kong a year before. A fishing boat had been found to be carrying 295 pounds of cocaine. The smugglers had gotten away but the navigator of the boat had identified several of them. To the agents' delight, the navigator said he would testify in court.

Madonna and Pritchard went to Hong Kong. Their job was to see if they could connect any of the smugglers to someone controlling the operation.

They started checking phone records and found that one of the smugglers made calls to a fur salesman named Johnny Kon. A look at Kon's business records showed he was selling more than coats. Several people listed as salesmen were known drug smugglers. Finally, the agents felt they knew who was in charge of the smuggling operation.

Back in Seattle, Tommy Chen was found guilty of smuggling heroin into the country and was sentenced to twenty years in federal prison. He never named Kon nor anyone else in the smuggling operation.

As Chen began to serve his sentence, Madonna and Pritchard started to look for as much proof as they could find against Johnny Kon.

A Witness Turns Against Kon

At 8 P.M. on January 19, 1986, Richard LaMagna of the DEA got a call from a customs agent at

New York's Kennedy Airport. A fifty-two-year-old Chinese woman had been arrested for trying to smuggle forty-four pounds of heroin into the country.

When LaMagna arrived at Kennedy, he saw that the heroin had been concealed inside large metal picture frames. The frames were supposed to be delivered to a hotel in midtown Manhattan. The woman was very well spoken and educated, and she seemed to be very upset that heroin had been found in the picture frames. She swore she didn't know anything about it.

The woman told the police she was to take the frames to the hotel and wait for a phone call. LaMagna and other agents from the DEA went with the woman to the hotel. LaMagna told the woman to talk calmly to the person who called and tell him or her to come to the hotel. The men from DEA would take it from there.

After waiting in the hotel room for two hours, the phone rang. Calmly, the woman picked up the receiver. Then suddenly she began yelling in Chinese into the phone. LaMagna and the other agents may not have understood Chinese but they knew she was telling the person on the other end that she had been arrested.

LaMagna grabbed the phone from her hand and slammed it down. The woman had tricked him. Once the phone was taken from her, the woman became silent. She was taken away.

LaMagna was angry. It could have been a perfect setup to catch part of a drug-smuggling ring from the Far East. At the same time, something about what had just happened in the hotel nagged at his memory.

The next morning LaMagna went through the files in his desk of other DEA arrests. When he read about an arrest in Seattle involving 138 metal ice buckets seven months earlier, he was amazed at the similarities between the two cases. LaMagna placed a call to Seattle.

In Seattle, DEA Agent Ed Madonna picked up the phone. Madonna listened to LaMagna's story of the woman with heroin in the metal picture frames. Then he told LaMagna about Tommy Chen. The drug-smuggling ring was even larger than anyone had thought. It was time for everyone to join forces.

LaMagna went to his boss to outline the case. Catherine Palmer was a United States attorney with the Justice Department. She listened to LaMagna's story. She gave LaMagna the full co-operation of the Justice Department.

Now Madonna, Pritchard, and LaMagna were pursuing leads to connect Johnny Kon to as many smugglers as they could. At the same time they were sure that Kon was still smuggling heroin into the United States.

There was bad news in June. The navigator of the fishing boat who had identified several of the smugglers had been found dead. What was worse, he had been killed in front of his family. The agents now knew Johnny Kon would stop at nothing to keep people from testifying against him in court.

For the next several months the investigation grew cold. There were just no leads. Then Madonna got another phone call from officials at the Seattle Airport.

A male passenger from Taiwan had tried to enter the country using a fake passport. When Madonna heard the man's name was Ah-ling his heart stopped. He was known by the agents to be one of Kon's smugglers. Madonna practically flew to the airport.

Records showed that Ah-ling had made almost twenty visits to the United States in the past two years. He often declared metal vases, and one time he had entered the country in the company of Fang Han-Sheng.

At first, Ah-ling denied any knowledge of Kon, Han-Sheng, or a drug-smuggling operation. But then Madonna slowly read off the dates of Ah-ling's trips to America, when he traveled with Han-Sheng, and how many metal vases he had brought into the country.

Ah-ling knew he had been caught. Slowly, he sat down and began to shake. In a quiet voice, he agreed to help the agents.

Yes, he knew Kon and Han-Sheng. Ah-ling admitted he smuggled heroin for Kon. He also told the agents that Kon had Han-Sheng killed after the ice buckets had been seized in Seattle. Ah-ling showed Madonna a photograph of Kon he had in his briefcase.

LaMagna flew out to Seattle. He and Madonna then asked Ah-ling to do something very dangerous, more dangerous than just testifying in court. The agents wanted Ah-ling to go undercover. Ah-ling would go back to Kon, learn about all his routes for smuggling heroin into the country, and help the agents put an end to this huge smuggling operation.

Ah-ling agreed even though he knew if Kon found out, he would be killed.

The Con to Get Kon

Ah-ling went back to Hong Kong and met with Agent Pritchard. Looking through photos the DEA agent had, Ah-ling was able to identify almost every smuggler that worked for Kon.

But there was a problem. For some reason, Kon was giving Ah-ling the cold shoulder. He wasn't asking him to do any more smuggling. Madonna worried that Kon might be on to their plan. But then why hadn't Ah-ling been killed? All the agents could do was wait for Kon to contact Ah-ling.

In the meantime, with the information Ah-ling had given Pritchard, DEA agents were starting to arrest smugglers as they tried to enter the United States. Even though the smugglers wouldn't talk, they could be held for smuggling heroin into the country.

Finally in April of 1987, Kon called Ah-ling and told him to come to Singapore. Madonna, La-Magna, and Pritchard all crossed their fingers that their witness was not being called there to be murdered. So did Ah-ling.

The meeting with Kon in Singapore did not begin well. There were several men in the hotel suite where the meeting was being held. Kon started the meeting by saying he knew there was a traitor among their group, and that one of the smugglers who had been arrested was now talking. He vowed to find that smuggler and have him killed.

Ah-ling began to grow nervous. He hoped it didn't show. Then Kon began to tell the men in the hotel that he was changing the way business was done. From now on, said Kon, they would be smuggling larger amounts of heroin into the States. That would cut down on the number of trips and the number of times the smugglers could be caught. The first such trip would be done by boat.

Kon turned to Ah-ling. It would be his job to find buildings in America where large amounts of heroin could be stored safely. In the meantime, Kon would begin to purchase heroin and store it in Thailand before sending it to the States. Kon planned to ship one ton of heroin to the West Coast of America by boat.

Ah-ling was relieved when he walked out of the hotel alive. Kon didn't know that he was working for the DEA. Returning to Hong Kong, Ah-ling met with Pritchard and told him of Kon's plans. He also warned the DEA agent that Kon was determined to kill the woman that had been arrested with the heroin-filled picture frames. She was a valuable witness, and the DEA was holding her in New York.

Catherine Palmer placed the witness under a protection program. The attorney then began to draw up indictments against Kon so that when he was finally arrested there would be evidence that would put him in jail immediately without bail.

Another smuggler was caught in September of 1987 when he was trying to bring in his own shipment of heroin. He had worked for Kon in the past and agreed to work with DEA agents in capturing him.

The agents were still trying to catch Kon before the one-ton shipment of heroin left for the United States. But Kon seemed to be able to travel throughout the Far East without being caught. Because he disguised himself, it became a cat-and-mouse chase with the mouse always getting away.

Then the agents got their break. Kon called Ah-ling. He needed to raise cash to buy more heroin. Since his smugglers had been getting arrested and the heroin taken into custody, he was not getting his money from the people who were buying heroin in the United States. Kon had to sell some property he owned in New York to raise cash.

Kon told Ah-ling to go to New York, sell the property, and bring the money back to him. Kon figured the property was worth twenty million dollars.

Ah-ling went to New York and met with Madonna and LaMagna. They had a plan.

Ah-ling was to return to Hong Kong and tell

Kon he had buyers for the property, but that the buyers insisted on meeting the owner before making any payments. This would get Kon to New York where the agents planned to grab him.

Ah-ling followed the instructions of the agents. When he told Kon he had buyers who insisted on meeting him, Kon didn't like the idea. He resisted going to New York. For a while it didn't look as if the plan was going to work.

Finally, Kon agreed to make the trip. He needed the money so he could buy more drugs. Kon called and said he would meet Ah-ling in New York on March 13, 1988, at 8 P.M. at the Hilton Hotel. The agents began to plan how they would grab Kon.

Sunday, March 13, was cold in New York. Gusts of wind made it even colder. Throughout the ground floor of the Hilton Hotel in midtown Manhattan, DEA agents lurked in doorways. They all had seen pictures of Kon and were to keep him in their sight.

In the bar off the lobby, Madonna sat at a table with LaMagna. They tried to look like regular hotel guests enjoying a drink. At a nearby table, another agent, Kevin Donnelly, sat by himself. All the agents were nervous.

They expected Kon to show with several bodyguards who would be carrying guns. The last thing the agents wanted was a shootout in a crowded hotel.

Ah-ling sat alone at a corner table. He, like the agents, was getting nervous — especially when Kon didn't show up at the scheduled time of 8 P.M.

Fingers began to tap nervously on several tables in the bar.

Suddenly Madonna looked up to see a well-dressed Chinese man walk into the bar as if searching for someone. To his amazement, the man seemed to be alone. When the Chinese man saw Ah-ling in the corner, he motioned for Ah-ling to join him in the restaurant. Madonna knew that the man was Johnny Kon.

After watching Ah-ling and Kon enter the restaurant, the three agents went into action. They took a table in the restaurant by the front door. Their table wasn't close to where Ah-ling and Kon sat. Though they couldn't hear the conversation, the agents could watch the table without Kon suspecting he was being watched.

Kon and Ah-ling talked as they ate dinner. Everything seemed normal. An hour after they sat down, Kon got up by himself. He put on his coat and walked out of the restaurant. The three agents jumped up from their table and followed.

Kon was about a block away from the Hilton when Agent Donnelly pulled out his gun, grabbed Kon, and told him he was under arrest. Kon remained calm. He said his name was Mr. Wong.

Putting handcuffs on Kon, the agents put him in a car and took him to DEA headquarters. The prisoner kept insisting his name was Wong.

Back at DEA headquarters, Madonna called Pritchard in Hong Kong. Now that Kon was in custody, Pritchard went about arresting all of Kon's contacts in Hong Kong. Suppliers of heroin as well as smugglers soon found themselves behind bars.

The next morning, Kon was taken to a federal courthouse in Brooklyn. Kon stood before the judge feeling sure that the agents didn't have enough proof to hold him. He was certain he would soon be on his way back to Hong Kong.

Then Catherine Palmer stood up and began reading off to the judge the charges against Kon. His confidence vanished as she listed not only several drug busts that could be traced back to Kon, but the names of the men who had been arrested in Hong Kong the night before.

The judge denied Kon bail. He would be kept in jail. Suddenly Kon's confident air turned to anger and hate. He turned to Agent Donnelly and told him that he would be killed.

The agent didn't believe him, until the DEA later learned of a plot to kidnap Donnelly and kill him. Kon's anger was also directed toward Catherine Palmer. Several months later she received a briefcase at her office. Luckily, agents stopped her before she opened it. Inside was a sawed-off rifle rigged to shoot whoever opened the briefcase.

Back in Hong Kong, the remaining smugglers and heroin sellers who worked for Kon and didn't get caught by the DEA ran off in different directions. Their leader was gone.

For more than a year, Kon tried to get his freedom. But finally, in September of 1989, Kon admitted his guilt to each count against him. He was sentenced to twenty-seven years in federal prison.

LaMagna and Palmer continue to bust drug smugglers from the Far East. They have been very successful but their battle requires constant vigilance.

Pritchard got married soon after Kon was arrested. He took his new wife to Seattle for their honeymoon. There, he and Agent Madonna had their own celebration.

They lifted their glasses of champagne and drank a toast to the end of Johnny Kon.